Essential Science

All about Gases

Peter Riley

W
FRANKLIN WATTS
LONDON • SYDNEY

First published in 2006 by Franklin Watts
338 Euston Road, London NW1 3BH

Franklin Watts Australia
Hachette Children's Books
Level 17/207 Kent Street, Sydney NSW 2000

Text copyright © Peter Riley 2006
Design and concept © Franklin Watts 2006

Editor: Rachel Tonkin
Designer: Proof Books
Picture researcher: Diana Morris
Illustrations: Ian Thompson

Picture credits:
Sonda Davies/Image Works/Topfoto: 10tr; David M. Dennis/OSF:
13t; Geri Engberg/Image Works/Topfoto: 5; Warren
Faidley/Photolibrary: 17; Silvio Fiore/Topfoto: 19t; Christopher
Fitzgerald/Image Works/Topfoto: 14; Robert Holmes/Corbis: 4t;
KMC International/Photolibrary: 12bl; Doug Lee/Still Pictures:
cover br,16; Moar/Topfoto: 24t; Plainpicture/Photolibrary: 15t;
Michael Pole/Corbis: 9; Alan Schein/Corbis: 4b;
Paul Seheult/Eye Ubiquitous/Corbis: 7c; Lee Snider/Image
Works/Topfoto: 24b; Joe Sohm/Image Works/Topfoto: 22b;
Westend61/Alamy: cover cr; David Woods/Corbis: 10bl.

All other images: Andy Crawford

With thanks to our model: Liam Cheung

A CIP catalogue record for this book
is available from the British Library

ISBN-10: 0 7496 6443 6
ISBN-13: 978 0 7496 6443 5

Dewey Classification: 533

Printed in China

CONTENTS

ALL ABOUT GASES

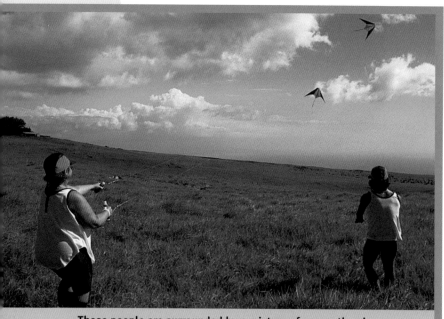

These people are surrounded by a mixture of gases: the air blows on the kites and makes them fly.

Gases are all around us. There are many different types including the gases in the air that we breathe in and out, and gas we cook with. There are also other gases, such as car exhaust fumes.

What are the gases of the air?

The gases of the air are: oxygen, nitrogen, carbon dioxide, water vapour, helium, neon, argon, krypton and xenon. Some of these are used or made when we breathe.

Can gases be seen?

Most gases do not have a colour and cannot be seen. Two gases that are coloured are chlorine, which is green, and bromine, which is brown. These gases are poisonous.

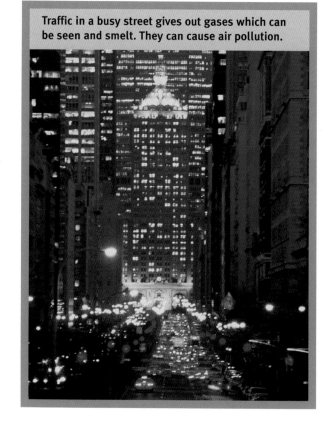

Traffic in a busy street gives out gases which can be seen and smelt. They can cause air pollution.

Do gases smell?

Some substances release gases which stimulate sensors in our noses. We say that these gases smell. Flowers release gases called scents which are pleasant smells. When food goes bad, for example rotten eggs, it releases gases that have unpleasant smells.

Flowers produce scent to attract insects. The insects help the plants reproduce by carrying their pollen from flower to flower.

Is a gas like a solid or a liquid?

A solid has a certain size and shape; a gas does not. When you press an aerosol can, such as an air freshner, a gas simply escapes into the air and spreads out. When you pump up a bicycle tyre you squeeze air very strongly to force it in. Liquids flow and so do gases. The wind is a strong flow of air.

Use the data

When scientists do experiments, they make observations and record them. This information is called data. It may be in the form of a table, bar chart or line graph. Collect some data about the use of gases in your home by answering questions like these.

How many things use natural gas? How many aerosol sprays are used? How many perfumes do people use? Make a bar chart like the one shown here. How does your bar chart compare?

You will find data on many pages in this book. Answers to all the questions in this book are on page 31.

THE AIR

The air covers the surface of the Earth and reaches out into space for 1,000 kilometres. You might think that air does not weigh anything, but it does. The weight of the air pushes down on us and is known as air pressure.

Showing that air has weight

You can show that the air has weight using a simple balance made from two balloons and a coat hanger. When you blow up, or inflate, a balloon, lots of air goes into it. If you tie an inflated balloon to one end of a coat hanger and an uninflated balloon to the other end, you will find that the end with the inflated balloon is pulled down. The weight of the air in the balloon pulls down the coat hanger.

The inflated balloon is heavier than the uninflated balloon.

Where air pressure comes from

You can think of layers of air like a pile of soft fluffy towels in an airing cupboard. As the towels are piled up, the ones at the bottom are squashed flatter by the weight of the towels above them. In a similar way the weight of the higher layers of air push down on the lower layers. This push of the air above us is known as air pressure.

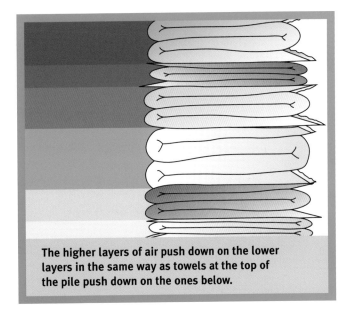

The higher layers of air push down on the lower layers in the same way as towels at the top of the pile push down on the ones below.

The change in air pressure makes the arrow on this barometer move to show how the weather will change.

Air pressure and weather

The air moves over the surface of the Earth and as it does so its pressure changes. Scientists who study the weather have found that when the air pressure is high the weather is often still with clear skies. This makes the weather warm in summer and cold in winter. When the air pressure is low the weather is windy and wet at any time of year. A barometer measures changes in air pressure and is used to predict the weather.

Predicting the weather

A barometer has a scale measuring air pressure in millibars (mb). It also has words describing the weather, such as rain, fair and change.

1 What is the air pressure shown by the barometer?
2 What weather do you predict if the pressure falls?
3 What weather do you predict if the pressure rises?

GASES FOR LIVING

Animals and plants need oxygen to get energy from food. Plants also need carbon dioxide to make their own food.

Living things and energy

Living things need energy to survive. They get their energy from food in a process called respiration. This takes place all over their bodies, all the time. In respiration, the body uses up oxygen and produces carbon dioxide.

Plants need carbon dioxide

Plants not only produce carbon dioxide, they use it as well. In daylight they take in large quantities of carbon dioxide and use it with water from the soil to make food. Some energy from sunlight is collected by the green leaves and stored in the food. The food-making process is called photosynthesis and the food is used by the plants and the animals that eat them.

Plants and oxygen

Plants also make oxygen when they make food. They make more oxygen than they need for respiration and release the excess into the air. This oxygen is then used by animals for respiration.

Oxygen

Carbon dioxide

Gases in water

Gases can dissolve in water. Aquatic animals (animals that live in water) take in oxygen dissolved in the water and give out carbon dioxide, which also dissolves in water. Plants in the water take in the dissolved carbon dioxide to use in photosynthesis and give out oxygen. This may sometimes be in the form of bubbles, but some of the oxygen leaves the bubbles and dissolves in the water.

When water splashes and forms bubbles, oxygen trapped in the bubbles dissolves in the water and can be used by aquatic plants and animals for respiration.

How the gases move around

Plants have tiny holes in the surfaces of their leaves which the gases can pass through. Carbon dioxide passes in and oxygen passes out. Most animals have special organs for taking in oxygen and giving out carbon dioxide as they breathe. Aquatic animals, such as fish, have gills. Animals that live on land, such as humans, have lungs. Oxygen from plants passes into the air or water and then into the lungs or gills of animals. Carbon dioxide from animals passes into the air and then into the leaves of plants. Plants and animals survive by exchanging oxygen and carbon dioxide.

Chemical equations

Scientists use chemical equations to explain how processes work. Here are two equations. Can you fill in the missing words.

Respiration
Oxygen + food → .... + water

Photosynthesis
Carbon dioxide + water → .... + food

USEFUL GASES

Many different gases are used every day for useful things. A gas can be used to cook your food, make fizzy drinks and even save you life in a road accident.

Oxygen

Oxygen is an important gas for life but it also has many other uses. Oxygen makes many things burn when they get hot enough (see page 22). The heat can be used to perform a useful task, such as welding. When a gas called acetylene is burnt with oxygen, so much heat is produced that the flame can cut through metal or weld it together.

This flame produced by burning oxygen and acetylene is so hot that it can melt metal.

This crash test dummy shows how the inflated airbag will protect the driver from being hurt.

Nitrogen

Nitrogen is used to inflate the air bags in a car. When a car crashes at more than 30 km per hour, a chemical reaction takes place in the air bags which produces a large amount of nitrogen. The nitrogen instantly fills the air bags and stops the driver and passengers hitting the inside of the car and badly injuring themselves.

Carbon dioxide

Things will not burn in carbon dioxide so it is used in some fire extinguishers. Carbon dioxide is also used in bread making. Yeast in the bread dough feeds on sugar in the flour and produces bubbles of carbon dioxide in the dough. At a fizzy drinks factory, carbon dioxide is dissolved in drinks such as lemonade to make them fizzy. When a can of fizzy drink is opened, the carbon dioxide escapes into the air, making the drink fizz and bubble.

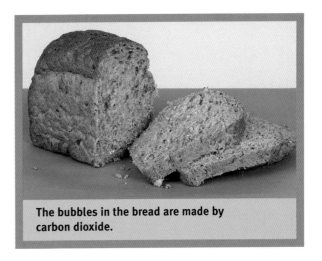

The bubbles in the bread are made by carbon dioxide.

The bubbles are made by carbon dioxide escaping from the drink when you open the can.

Natural gas

Natural gas formed from the bodies of sea creatures which died millions of year ago. It collected in spaces in rocks. It is extracted and is piped into houses where it is used to heat homes and cook food. If the gas leaks it can be dangerous because it will burn with oxygen in the air and cause a fire. Natural gas does not have a smell so smelly gases, called mercaptans, are added to it so you can tell if natural gas is leaking.

What makes dough rise

Four lumps of dough were prepared. The table shows what they contained, where they were put and how much they rose due to carbon dioxide gas being produced.

1 What does the dough need to contain for it to rise?
2 How does warmth or coldness affect how much the dough rises?
3 Predict the result for the empty box in the table.

Dough	Contents	Place	Dough rose by (mm)
A	flour sugar yeast	warm	20
B	flour sugar	warm	0
C	flour sugar yeast	cold	5
D	flour sugar	cold	

AIR SPACES

Many substances that we call solids actually have small spaces in them which are filled with air.

Sponge

The air spaces in a sponge can easily be seen. When a sponge is squashed, the air spaces get smaller and the air is forced out but you cannot see the air moving. If the sponge is placed in water and squashed, the air can be seen leaving the sponge because it forms bubbles.

The bubbles have formed from air squashed out of the sponge.

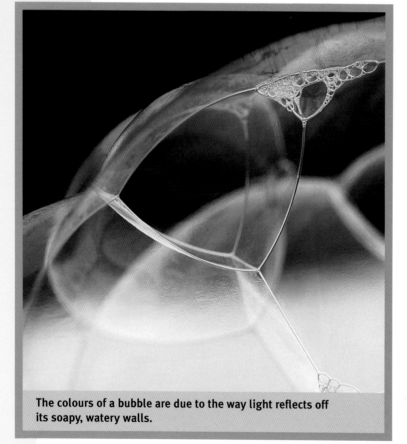

The colours of a bubble are due to the way light reflects off its soapy, watery walls.

Soap bubbles

When bubbles rise to the surface of water they break through the surface and pop. The air in them mixes with the air above the water. If soap is added to the water the bubble can push the water up until it makes a sphere with thin walls of water. If the soap bubble rises into the air, it can seem to have all the colours of the rainbow.

Soil

Soil is made from particles which only fit loosely together. This allows air spaces to form between the particles.

As the earthworm moves along its burrow, it takes in oxygen from the air and makes holes in the earth which let the air mix with the soil.

The oxygen in the air is used by tiny living things in the soil and by plant roots.

The amount of air in the soil can be found in the following way. Fill a beaker with soil and a measuring cylinder with water. Write down the amount of water in the measuring cylinder. Then, pour the water slowly from the measuring cylinder onto the soil. When the water appears at the surface of the soil, all the air spaces have been filled. You can work out the volume of air in the air spaces in the soil. Look at how much water is left in the measuring cylinder then subtract this amount from the amount of water that was in the measuring cylinder at the start of the experiment.

Water on soil soon drains into it to fill up the air spaces.

The air in three soils

The table shows the amount of water in measuring cylinders at the start and after testing different soils.

1 What was the volume of the air spaces in soils A, B and C?

2 Which soil would you expect to have the most tiny living organisms and which would you expect to have the least?

Soil	Volume at start (cm^3)	Volume at end (cm^3)
A	50	39
B	50	45
C	50	32

EVAPORATION

During a shower of rain, puddles form on the ground, but as the rain stops and the clouds clear, the puddles gradually shrink and disappear. This is due to a process called evaporation.

Why puddles shrink

The water at the surface of a puddle evaporates. In this process, liquid water changes into a gas called water vapour. It is colourless, does not smell and mixes with the air. When some of the water has evaporated there is less left behind. This makes the puddle smaller.

If there is no more rain, this puddle will eventually disappear altogether.

Blowing in the wind

If you hang out washing on a still day it dries slowly. This happens because the water that has evaporated from the washing stays close to its surface. It blocks the way for more water vapour to leave the surface and the washing takes a long time to dry.

When the air is moving, as on a windy day, the water vapour that has evaporated is blown away so more water can evaporate from the washing. This means that windy days are the best days for drying washing.

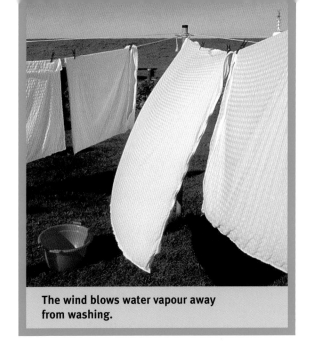

The wind blows water vapour away from washing.

Evaporation and energy

Energy is needed for water to evaporate. On a cloudy day, warmth in the air provides the energy for evaporation to take place. On a sunny day, the heat in the Sun's rays provides more energy for evaporation. This means that puddles dry up faster and washing dries faster on a sunny day.

Three containers of water with different surface areas were left for a day to allow evaporation to take place.

The effect of surface area

The volume of water in three containers (see above) was measured at the start of an experiment and again at the end to see how much the water had evaporated.

Container	Surface area (cm^2)	First vol area (cm^3)	Second vol area (cm^3)
Bowl	400	1000	700
Jug	200	1000	900
Bottle	25	1000	950

1 How much water was lost by evaporation in each container?

2 How does the size of the surface area seem to affect the amount of water that evaporates?

GASES ON THE MOVE

Gases can move through each other by diffusion. Heat also creates small volumes of moving air called air currents. Larger volumes of moving air are called winds.

The hot air in the balloon rises above the colder air around it.

Diffusion

If you put an air freshener in a room and close the door, when you return the whole room will smell of the scent. This is due to a process called diffusion. Pleasant-smelling substances in the air freshener evaporate into the air and then slowly mix with it. As they mix they spread out so that in time the whole room smells pleasant. If there is a gas leak, the gas spreads out in the air by diffusion, too, and the unpleasant-smelling mercaptans (see page 11) mean you can smell the gas.

Air currents

If you put your hand over a warm surface, such as an electric heater, you can feel the warm air pushing against your hand. When air gets warm it becomes lighter than the cooler air around it. This makes it rise. The cooler air takes the place of the rising air and in turn becomes warm. It then rises, too, and is replaced by more of the cooler air. These air currents produce a circling current of air called a convection current.

Breezes

When the Sun shines on land and sea, the land warms up faster than the water. The land heats the air above it and the air rises. Air moves in from the sea to replace the rising air and makes a sea breeze. At night, the water cools down more slowly than the land. The air above the sea rises and the air above the land moves out over the sea to replace it and makes a land breeze.

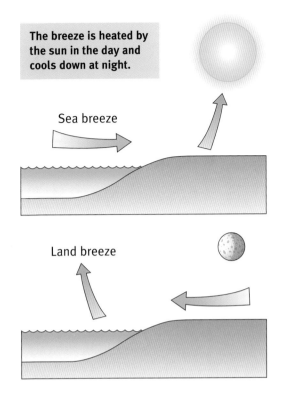

The breeze is heated by the sun in the day and cools down at night.

Sea breeze

Land breeze

Hurricane winds swirl the clouds round into a huge disc.

Winds

Winds are stronger than breezes. They form in the same way – by large volumes of cooler air rushing to replace large amounts of rising warmer air. When some oceans become warm, huge amounts of air rise above them and winds swirl round to replace them. They form a hurricane.

Wind speed

The Beaufort wind scale can be used to estimate wind speed. Over a week, note down how the wind feels each day and use this table to compare their change in strength.

Force	Effect	Speed (km/h)	Description
0	smoke rises sraight up	0	calm
1–4	leaves rustle	1–29	moderate winds
5–7	large trees sway	30–61	strong breeze
8–11	difficult to walk	62–119	strong gale
12	severe damage caused	120+	hurricane

BOILING AND CONDENSING

When any liquid is heated it eventually reaches a temperature at which it boils. The liquid turns very quickly into a gas by evaporation and mixes with the air. If the temperature of the gas falls, it forms a liquid again by condensation.

Bringing to the boil

When a liquid is heated its temperature rises steadily. Eventually the temperature stops rising. At this temperature the liquid is boiling and the temperature is called the boiling point. The boiling point of water is 100 °C.

In evaporation (see page 14), water vapour escapes from the surface of a liquid at a temperature below its boiling point. When water boils, the water vapour forms below the liquid's surface and makes bubbles.

Water vapour in the bubbles is lighter than the water around them so the bubbles rise to the surface.

If you keep heating a boiling liquid its temperature does not rise any more, the liquid just boils faster. As the liquid boils, its volume decreases as more of it turns into gas. Eventually all the liquid will boil away. When this happens the liquid is said to have boiled dry.

What is steam?

If you watch a kettle boil you will see white clouds form above its spout. The clouds are called steam but they are not real steam. The real steam forms just above the boiling water. It is water vapour at 100 °C. As the steam rushes out of the spout its temperature remains at 100 °C and it remains colourless which means it cannot be seen. When the steam moves away from the spout its temperature falls as it touches dust particles in the air. The steam changes back or condenses into a liquid again and forms a tiny droplet on each dust particle. The huge number of droplets scatter light in all directions and this makes them appear white. The clouds are really condensed

The force of steam as it pushes away from boiling water is used to move a steam locomotive.

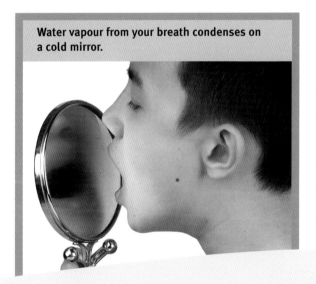

Water vapour from your breath condenses on a cold mirror.

Breathing out

The linings of your lungs and mouth are moist with water. When you breathe out, some of the water evaporates and leaves your body as water vapour in your breath. On cold days, if the water vapour meets cooler air it condenses and forms a white cloud.

Reading a graph

A pan of water was heated and its temperature recorded every minute.

1 How long did the water take to reach 60 °C?
2 What was the temperature of the water after four minutes?
3 How long did it take for the water to boil?

THE WATER CYCLE

Look for a cloud in the sky. In a few days you could be drinking the water in it.

1. From sea to clouds

A huge amount of water evaporates from the seas every day. It forms water vapour, which mixes with the other gases in the air. The Sun's heat warms the air above the seas and it rises carrying the water vapour with it. The air cools as it rises and the water vapour condenses on dust particles in the air to form clouds.

2. From clouds to rain

Clouds are blown along by the wind. When they are blown towards hills they rise up and cool down. The low temperature at the cloud tops makes the water droplets freeze and form snowflakes. They fall through the cloud, melt and form raindrops.

3. From soil to plant

Some of the rain that falls on soil is taken up by plants. They use some of the water to make food in their leaves but the rest evaporates inside the leaves and then passes out through the holes in their surfaces. The water vapour mixes with the air gases and may eventually condense to form clouds.

4. Into town and back to the sea

Most rainwater drains into rivers. Some water is collected behind dams and forms reservoirs. The water is drawn off from here out to houses, towns and cities. The rest of the water flows from the rivers back to the sea. This movement of water is the water cycle.

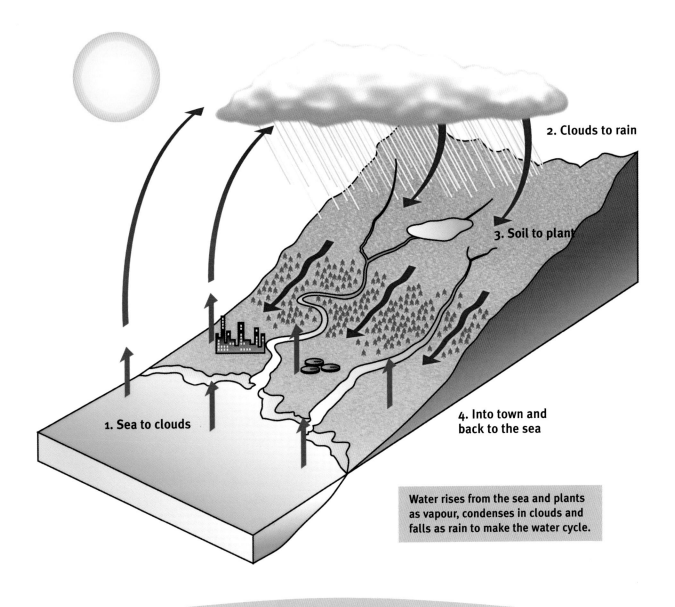

2. Clouds to rain

3. Soil to plant

1. Sea to clouds

4. Into town and back to the sea

Water rises from the sea and plants as vapour, condenses in clouds and falls as rain to make the water cycle.

How rainfall changes

The bar chart shows the rainfall in a certain place over 12 months.

1 How many months had rain?
2 In which month did most rain fall?
3 How did the rainfall change from March to June?
4 How did the rainfall change from September to December?

BURNING, RUSTING AND BUBBLING

Gases can cause things to burn or rust. When some solids and liquids are mixed together, a gas is made. These changes are irreversible.

Air and burning

You can investigate air and burning with a simple experiment. Put a candle on a saucer of water, light the candle and then place a glass over the top (see picture 1). The glass traps air over the candle. As the candle burns, the volume of air in the glass decreases by about a fifth. Water rises up inside the glass to replace it (see picture 2). The part of the air that is used up is oxygen. Almost all the rest is made from nitrogen, which does not let things burn in it.

1. The candle uses up the oxygen in the air in the glass.

2. The candle goes out as it has used up all the oxygen. The oxygen has been replaced by water.

Water and oxygen in the air have caused this old tractor to rust.

Rusting and oxygen

Rust is a reddish-brown substance that forms on the metals iron and steel when a chemical reaction takes place between the metal, oxygen and moisture. Things made of iron or steel that are left out in the open air rust because the moisture in the air reacts with oxygen and begins to corrode the metal.

Bubbling up

When some solids and liquids are mixed together, a chemical reaction takes place and new materials are formed. Sometimes one of the new materials is a gas. It forms bubbles in the liquid, which eventually pop and release the gas into the air.

For example, if vinegar and bicarbonate of soda are mixed, a chemical reaction takes place which produces bubbles of carbon dioxide gas.

This kind of change cannot be reversed like the processes of evaporation and condensation. It is an irreversible change.

You can make a vinegar volcano by adding a little red food dye to vinegar then pouring the mixture into a bottle containing bicarbonate of soda.

Burning in different sized jars

A burning candle was covered by three different-sized jars in turn and the time for the candle to go out was recorded. The experiment was repeated twice and the burning times are shown in columns T1, T2 and T3.

1 What is the total burning time for each jar?
2 What is the average burning time for each jar? (Divide the total by three).
3 Arrange the jars in order of size starting with the largest.

Jar	Burning time (secs)			Total time (secs)	Average (secs)
	T1	T2	T3		
A	30	33	30		
B	15	13	17		
C	25	27	26		

POLLUTING GASES

Some gases are harmful to the environment. Recently, more of these gases have been produced by traffic and factories. People are trying to reduce the amount of these gases being produced.

The wind can be used to turn turbines and generate electricity without producing harmful gases.

Carbon dioxide

When coal, oil or natural gas is burnt in power stations, a large amount of carbon dioxide is produced. Carbon dioxide is called a 'greenhouse gas'. It mixes with the air and makes the Earth's atmosphere behave like a greenhouse. Heat from the Sun passes through the Earth's atmosphere but greenhouse gases stop heat being reflected from the Earth and passing back into space.

As more greenhouse gases build up, more heat is trapped and temperatures rise. This is known as 'global warming'. It is thought to be causing icecaps to melt and changes in climate in many parts of the world. People are trying to find alternative power sources, such as wind, which do not produce carbon dioxide. However, there are many other sources of carbon dioxide, such as burning fuel in car and aeroplane engines.

Exhaust gases

When fuel is burnt in vehicle engines, harmful gases, such as nitrous oxide and carbon monoxide, are also produced. Nitrous oxide makes acid rain, which damages stone buildings, plants and fish in rivers. Carbon monoxide is deadly if large amounts are breathed in. Catalytic converters remove these harmful gases.

Sulphur dioxide gas from burning coal and nitrous oxide makes acid rain which damages stonework and kills life in rivers.

CFCs

Ozone is a naturally occurring gas which forms a layer in the atmosphere at a height of about 15–30 kilometres above the Earth's surface. The sun releases rays of ultraviolet light which are harmful to living things. Ozone absorbs most of these rays and protects life on Earth. CFCs are chemicals which contain chlorine and have been used for many years in aerosol sprays and in fridges. When these gases are released into the air the chlorine attacks the ozone layer. This has resulted in holes appearing in the ozone layer, which let in harmful rays from the Sun. New chemicals which do not contain chlorine are now used in aerosols and fridges so this will help protect the ozone layer.

Aerosols now contain chemicals which do not attack the ozone layer.

Sulphur dioxide pollution

The amount of sulphur dioxide in the air is measured in parts per million (ppm). This means if the ppm is 6 there are six particles of sulphur dioxide in 1 million particles of air. Here are the amounts of sulphur dioxide in a town measured over a week.

1 On which days was the pollution the lowest?
2 How did the pollution level change from Monday to Tuesday?
3 How much did it change from Tuesday to Wednesday?

GASES, SOLIDS AND LIQUIDS

Everything in the universe is made from solids, liquids or gases. How do solids and liquids compare with gases?

States of matter

Scientists divide all substances into solids, liquids and gases. They call them the three states of matter. Each state has properties which are different to the other two.

Solids

- A solid has a definite shape and volume.
- A solid has mass and weight.
- Tiny fragments of solids, such as grains of sand, can be poured.
- Solids form when liquids freeze.
- Most solids cannot be squashed. However, when a solid, such as a sponge, is squashed, you simply squeeze out the air. The volume of the actual sponge stays the same.

Liquids

- A liquid has a definite volume.
- Liquids have mass and weight.
- Liquids can flow.
- A liquid takes up the shape of the container in which it is placed.
- When liquids freeze they become solids.
- When liquids evapourate they become gases.
- When a liquid changes its shape, the volume stays the same.
- You cannot squash a liquid.

Gases

- A gas does not have a definite shape or volume.
- Gases have mass and weight.
- Gases can flow and be squashed.
- Gases form when liquids evaporate or boil.

What is matter made from?

It is easy to see what solids and liquids are made from. Your can feel the shape and surface of a solid and let a harmless liquid run over your hands. It is difficult to imagine what gases are made from because you cannot usually see or touch them like solids and liquids. Scientists have discovered that all states of matter are made from tiny particles, which are too small to see.

In solids, the particles stick together like bricks in a wall. In liquids, the particles can slide over each other when the liquid is poured. In gases the particles are free to move around in all directions and can crash into each other and any surfaces around them.

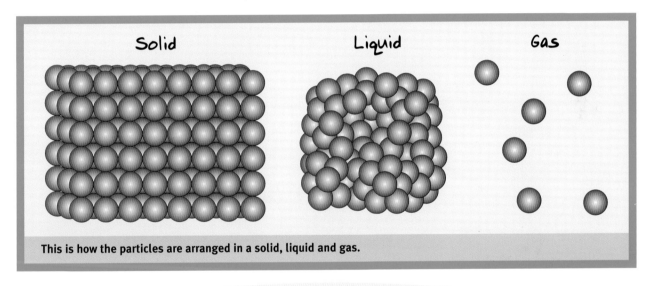

This is how the particles are arranged in a solid, liquid and gas.

What is the substance?   Which substances are a solid, liquid or gas?

Substance	Fixed shape	Definite volume	Melts when heated
A	No	Yes	No
B	No	No	No
C	Yes	Yes	Yes
D	No	Yes	No
E	No	No	No

CAN YOU REMEMBER THE ESSENTIALS?

Here are the essential science facts about gases. They are set out in the order you can read about them in the book. Spend a couple of minutes learning each set of facts. If you can learn them all, you know all the essentials about gases.

The air (pages 6-7)

Air has weight.
The push of the air is called air pressure.
Changes in air pressure produce changes in the weather.

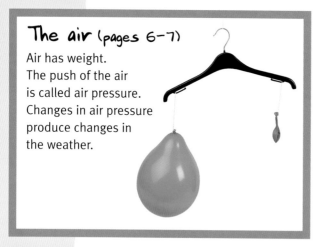

Useful gases (pages 10-11)

Oxygen is needed for burning to take place.
Natural gas is burnt for heating buildings and for cooking.

Carbon dioxide is used in fire extinguishers, fizzy drinks and to make bread spongy.
Nitrogen is used in air bags.

Vital gases (pages 8-9)

Living things need oxygen for respiration.
Carbon dioxide is produced during respiration.
Plants make food in a process called photosynthesis.
Plants use carbon dioxide in photosynthesis.
Plants produce oxygen in photosynthesis.

Air spaces (pages 12-13)

Air spaces are found in sponges.
Bubbles in water are formed by a gas.
Air spaces are found in soil.
The volume of air in the air spaces of soil can be found by measuring the amount of water poured into soil to fill them.

Evaporation (pages 14–15)

When a liquid evaporates it changes into a gas.
When water evaporates it changes into a gas called water vapour.
Wind, warmth and increased surface area speed up evaporation.

Gases on the move (pages 16–17)

Gases can move through each other by a process called diffusion.
Air can flow and make currents and winds.
Air currents are made when part of the air is warmer than the rest.

Boiling and condensing (pages 18–19)

If a liquid is heated, its temperature will rise until it boils.
The temperature at which a liquid boils is called its boiling point.

Heating a boiling liquid makes it boil faster.
Steam is a colourless gas at 100 ºC.
When a gas cools down it may condense and change into a liquid.

The water cycle (pages 20–21)

Huge amounts of water evaporate into the air from the sea.
Clouds form when water vapour high in the air condenses.
When clouds cool enough rain falls from them.
Water returns to the sea along rivers.

Burning, rusting and bubbling (pages 22–23)

About a fifth of the air is made from oxygen.
Oxygen is needed for burning to take place.
Oxygen and water are needed for iron to rust.

Gases can be made when some irreversible changes take place between solids and liquids.

Polluting gases (pages 24–25)

Carbon dioxide produces the greenhouse effect in the atmosphere.
Increased carbon dioxide in the atmosphere may be causing global warming.
The ozone layer protects living things from harmful rays.
CFCs have made holes in the ozone layer.
Some gases make acid rain.
Ways are being found to reduce the amounts of harmful gases.

Gases, solids and liquids (pages 26–27)

Solid, liquid and gas are the three states of matter.
Gases do not have a definite shape.
Gases do not have a definite volume.
Gases can flow.
Gases can be squashed.
Gases have mass and weight.

GLOSSARY

Air pressure The push of the air on everything around it.

Aerosol can A container which has a large amount of gas squeezed inside it as a liquid. When the top is pressed the gas sends a spray of liquid out.

Atmosphere The mixture of gases that surrounds a planet or moon.

Barometer A device which measures air pressure.

Boiling The process in which a liquid changes into a gas at its boiling point.

Condensation The process in which a gas turns into a liquid when it cools.

Convection currents Currents of air which are involved in the transport of heat.

Dam A huge wall built across a river to stop the flow of water and build up a reservoir behind it.

Diffusion A process in which one substance spreads out in another substance and mixes with it.

Dissolve A process in which a substance separates and spreads out through a liquid and seems to disappear into it.

Dough A mixture of flour, water and yeast.

Energy Something which allows an object or a living thing to take part in an activity such as moving or making a noise.

Evaporation A process in which a liquid changes into a gas at a temperature below the boiling point of the liquid.

Lungs Organs in many air-breathing animals where oxygen in the air enters the animal's blood and carbon dioxide in the blood enters the air.

Mass The amount of matter in a substance.

Organ A structure in the body that performs a particular task.

Reservoir A place where water is stored to supply buildings such as homes, schools and factories.

Sensors Ends of nerves which detect changes.

Sewage works The place where solid and liquid wastes from toilets are made harmless. The liquid can then be released into a river and the solid can be used as fertiliser to grow plants.

Steam The gas form of water at 100 °C.

Ultra-violet light Rays of light we cannot see but large amounts can burn our skin.

Volume The space that is filled by a certain amount of matter.

Water vapour The gas form of water below 100°C.

Welding A process of joining metals together by melting them.

Wind farm A place where electricity is generated by using the wind to turn the blades of windmill-like turbines.

Yeast A substance used to make bread rise and form alcohol in beer and wine.

ANSWERS

The air (pages 6–7)
1 998 mb
2 It will rain.
3 It will be fine.

Gases for living (pages 8–9)
Respiration – Carbon dioxide
Photosynthesis – Oxygen

Useful gases (pages 10–11)
1 Flour, sugar and yeast.
2 Warmth makes the dough rise high. Coldness makes the dough rise only a little.
3 0.

Air spaces (pages 12–13)
1 A = 11 cm³; B = 5 cm³; C = 18 cm³.
2 C would have most and B would have least.

Evaporation (pages 14–15)
1 Bowl = 300 cm³; jug = 100 cm³;
bottle = 50 cm³.
2 The larger the surface area the more water evaporates.

Gases on the move (pages 16–17)
The answer will vary according to circumstances. Some children may give more detailed answers by estimating the wind speed not once a day but at different times in the day.

Boiling and condensing (pages 18–19)
1 2 minutes.
2 90 °C.
3 6 minutes.

The water cycle (pages 20–21)
1 10.
2 February.
3 The rainfall decreased.
4 The rainfall increased.

Burning, rusting and bubbling (pages 22–23)
1 A = 93; B = 45; C= 78
2 A = 31; B = 15; C = 26
3 A, C, B.

Polluting gases (Page 24 – 25)
1 Friday, Saturday, Sunday.
2 It went up 2 ppm.
3 It went down 3 ppm.

Gases, liquids and solids (page 26 – 27)
A = liquid; B = gas; C = solid; D = liquid; E = gas.

INDEX